*W*EDDING PHOTOGRAPHY

Getting the
Perfect
Pictures

GW00750531

JO PACKHAM

A Sterling/Chapelle Book
Sterling Publishing Co., Inc. New York

WEDDING
PHOTOGRAPHY

Jo Packham
Author

Cherie Hanson
Editor/Designer

Jackie McCowen
Editor

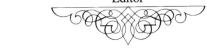

Library of Congress Cataloging-in-Publication Data

Packham, Jo.
    Wedding photography : getting the perfect pictures / Jo Packham.
        p.   cm.
    "A Sterling/Chapelle book."
    Includes index.
    ISBN 0-8069-0485-2
    1. Wedding photography.   I. Title.
  TR819.P33 1993
  778.9'93925—dc00   93–4674
                                                                          CIP

10 9 8 7 6 5 4 3 2 1

A Sterling/Chapelle Book

Published by Sterling Publishing Company, Inc.
387 Park Avenue South, New York, N.Y. 10016
© 1994 by Chapelle Ltd.
Distributed in Canada by Sterling Publishing
$^{c}/_{o}$ Canadian Manda Group, P.O. Box 920, Station U
Toronto, Ontario, Canada M8Z 5P9
Distributed in Great Britain and Europe by Cassell PLC
Villiers House, 41/47 Strand, London WC2N 5JE, England
Distributed in Australia by Capricorn Link (Australia) Pty Ltd.
P.O. Box 6651, Baulkham Hills, Business Centre, NSW 2153, Austra[l]
Manufactured in the United States of America

Sterling ISBN 0-8069-0485-2

Contents

Introduction

A picture is a poem without words.

—*Latin Proverb*

After months of planning, your wedding celebration will be over in a matter of hours and events will take place either that you did not see because you were busy elsewhere or that you simply will not remember. Memories can be forgotten in a day filled with a myriad of different emotions, a time when there are so many things to remember, and events that require what seem to be an infinite number of people to be gathered and taken care of. So, after all is said and done, all you will have to remember this joyous occasion by, other than a few selective memories and stories told to you by friends, are your wedding photographs. If taken to your specifications, nothing will bring you more pleasure over the years than these. It is true that amateurs, friends, and family can help you cut wedding costs by taking all of your photographs during the wedding ceremony and the reception, but please do not try to economize here. Remember, these pictures are treasures that will be handed down for generations. So, trust your picture taking only to a professional!

Selecting a Photographer

*All the flowers of all the tomorrows are
in the seeds of today.*

—*Author Unknown*

Long before you actually select your wedding
photographer, you will want to give special consider-
ation to the type of wedding photography you prefer.
Do you want a photographer who mingles with the
guests, captures candid shots, and unobtrusively
chronicles the events of the day; or do you prefer
photographs for your album that are a little more
formal and posed so that you know exactly what you
will be getting? There is no right or wrong style for
wedding photography—these pictures are your
images and your memories. They will become part of
your family history and be viewed for generations, so
they should be taken exactly as you want them taken.

To make certain you hire a reputable and talented photographer who will take the type of pictures that *you* want, you should begin interviewing at least five months before the scheduled wedding date. You will want to reserve your date as early as possible because photographers have seasons that are very busy and they may be booked as much as a year in advance. Christmas is always a chaotic time for photographers, as well as is autumn with senior pictures. June is also busy because of all of the weddings and graduations taking place. These and other such special dates can overbook a photographer.

You can select a photographer by using the following resources:

1. Ask family and friends for any recommendations. It is especially helpful if they have recently been involved with a wedding themselves.

2. Ask other wedding professionals (such as bridal-salon personnel, caterers, or florists) whom they might recommend.

3. Look in the Yellow Pages under "Photographers". The style of photographs that you prefer may, to some extent, dictate the kind of photographer you will interview. Some photographers are listed as wedding photographers, some as portraiture photographers, some as commercial photographers. Do not, however, be

influenced by the size of the ad in the Yellow Pages. Many of the best commercial or wedding photographers do not advertise. They will simply have their name and number in the directory, because most of their business is obtained by word of mouth—if they are very good, they are as busy as they want to be!

4. Ask at local bridal shows sponsored by the wedding coordinators and retailers in your area.

5. Contact Professional Photographers of America in Atlanta, Georgia, at 1-800-786-6277 for a list of professionals in your area.

Once you have selected three photographers, you will want to do the following:

1. Make an appointment with each photographer, and allow at least one hour to discuss the details. Take notes during the interviews because you will never be able to remember everything they say.

2. Make certain you ask each photographer whether he/she has a specialty. Most photographers who specialize in weddings concentrate on typical wedding photographs. If you want something out of the ordinary, you may not want to hire a wedding specialist but a commercial photographer to achieve your desires.

3. Make sure you inspect their portfolios, and sample albums, or visit their studios. Pay attention to details, such as clarity (focus), the richness in the colors of the photos, technical know-how, the creativity in both cropping and posing, as well as the naturalness of the subjects' positions. Check their lighting; it should be soft without harsh shadows or hot spots (glares). Do they use special techniques, such as soft-focus lenses, multiple exposures, or split framing, and do you want these techniques used? If a photographer particularly likes any special technique, you can almost be guaranteed that it will be used whether you want it or not! If you do not see

a particular style or setting in the photographer's portfolio, chances are high that he/she will not or cannot deliver such a special request for you—even if he/she promises to!

As well as inspecting their work, study their personalities. You want to select someone who has a pleasant personality, who will listen to what you want, and with whom you are comfortable. Some wedding photographers can be overbearing in their demands and offensive to guests and wedding party participants. This is the one provider of wedding services that you will spend more time with during the actual festivities than any other. You need to like and feel comfortable with this person. If something they do or say annoys you during the interview, or if you have trouble making them understand exactly what it is that you want, it will only be magnified during the actual festivities. At that time, there is much more pressure and many more emotions to contend with, so you must have complete faith in whomever you hire.

4. Show the photographers photographs that you have cut out of magazines and books that depict the look you want.

5. Inquire as to their wedding packages and what is included. Most photographers will have a brochure describing their services, policies, and package prices. You will want to check the following package details:

- Does the quoted price include a wedding album, and is the album embossed, leather, or vinyl?

- Are the pictures they have selected to include in the package the ones you really want?

- How much is the charge for additional pictures?

- Does the price compare to what would be charged if you had all of the single photographs taken that you want?

- What is the charge for additional photographs that will be wanted by you and other family members or wedding participants?

- Does the package fee include the cost of retouching the photos, or is this service additional?

- How many exposures does the package price include?

- How many candid shots are included in the quoted price?

- How is a new price determined if you add shots during the festivities?

- Does the package price state how long the photographer will stay at the wedding and/or the reception?

A typical package might include an 8" x 10" album for you and the groom, two 5" x 7" albums for both sets of parents, an 11" x 30" portrait, a selection of 5" x 7" prints for the bridal party and other family members, and some wallet-size photos that can be sent with thank-you cards.

If you are trying to save money on your photography, here are some places where you may be able to cut without giving up the idea of hiring a professional altogether.

- Purchase your album elsewhere at another time or ask for one as a gift. Simply pay the photographer for the pictures and put them together yourself.

- Consolidate your pictures when ordering them, and order as many multiples as you think you will possibly want or need. Second and third prints are much less expensive than first prints.

- Have the photographer take only the necessary pictures you want to have included in the album, and have family and friends take the candid shots. If they take enough, you will get some very good ones that will rekindle many fond memories.

6. Discuss other possible photographs with each photographer. For example, a formal pre-wedding picture of you to display at the reception, a photograph of you and the groom to include on your wedding invitations or thank-you notes, or a special photograph to give as a gift to parents or participants. If you are planning these or other pre-wedding photos, discuss them thoroughly with the photographer. Let him/her know the specific location, your attire, the style of makeup you plan on wearing, and so on. You may also want to have some of these special photographs taken in black-and-white or taken in black-and-white and hand-colored. These can be very dramatic and "arty," and may be the pictures you like more than any of the others.

7. Tell each photographer how many people are in the wedding party, the style of your wedding, your wedding colors, and any other pertinent information. For example, you do not want the photographer coming to what he/she expects will be a small, traditional wedding, only to find a very large, contemporary wedding, where you, as the bride, are dressed in red and your entourage of bridesmaids are all attired in different-colored ethnic dresses.

8. Tell each photographer the time of the ceremony and the reception and the locations for both (indoors or outdoors can make a great deal of difference to a photographer). Make certain he/she agrees to be the first to arrive and the last to leave, taking photographs the entire time. Some of the very early shots or the ones of everyone cleaning up after you have gone may be the most memorable in your album. Be certain to check this in regards to the package the photographer offers. Some will not stay the entire time and seem to speed up the events of the reception so that they can take all of the required shots in the allotted amount of time.

9. The photographer should visit both the ceremony and reception sites with you before your wedding day to check on the logistics. Discuss, with the church officiant, any restrictions for taking

photographs during certain times in certain locations, and make sure you arrange for any additional equipment that may be necessary.

10. Make sure the photographer will meet with you a day or two before the wedding. The purpose of this meeting is to give him/her a detailed list of the events you wish to have photographed and to introduce him/her to a close friend or family member who will identify important guests you want to be included in the photos. This is the person to whom the photographer can ask any questions during both the ceremony and the reception. The person you select will need to let the photographer know where he/she will be seated during the ceremony and be easily accessible during the reception.

11. Discuss the attire the photographer and any assistants will wear to the wedding so that it will be in keeping with the other wedding participants. If you request that their attire be something out of the ordinary, you will need to discuss who will pay for the rental or the purchase of the desired garments.

12. Ask each photographer if he/she will be the one who actually takes all of the photographs before and during your wedding rather than turning the actual work over to a less-experienced employee. Does he/she have assistants to help with the equipment and take additional shots elsewhere during the festivities?

13. Ask each photographer whether they carry an extra camera, just in case something goes wrong with the one he/she intends to use. If not, what is his/her solution to such a problem?

14. Discuss who actually owns the film and the proofs of the pictures taken for you. Proofs are usually 5" x 7" pictures that the photographer will give you to select from. They have not been retouched and should be numbered for ease in ordering. If the photographer does not ordinarily number the proofs, make certain there is some sort of system so that multiples can be ordered by several different parties without each needing to have the originals to present with their order.

Some photographers will not give you the negatives to have processed elsewhere. They maintain ownership and they are the only ones who may develop them. If they do retain ownership of the film, ask if there is an additional charge if you wish to keep the proofs. Inquire as to how long they will allow you to keep the proofs before you are required to return them with your decision and how long they keep them on file in case you want to reorder in ten years or so? Find out if they will give you the negatives after a certain time frame when they no longer wish to keep them in their files?

15. Discuss the fee. Is there a separate charge for film as well as time and travel to come to the ceremony and reception site to take the photos? Is there an additional charge for any pre-wedding meetings? Is one day of the week or time of day more expensive than others?

16. What kind of a deposit is required? It is a good idea to place your deposit on a credit card, protecting yourself by special consumer protection laws should something go wrong with the photographs you had agreed to.

17. If the cost is too high for your budget, perhaps you can work out a payment schedule with the photographer for the package or photographs you select. However, you will want to ask how any additional unplanned pictures will fit into the payment schedule. Even though you feel you only want a certain number now, undoubtedly there will be several pictures taken during the festivities that you will want after you see them.

18. Ask them about their cancellation policy—in regards to your cancelling or their cancelling. What is your recourse if, for example, the photographer calls three days before the wedding and says he/she simply will not be able to make it?

19. Get a detailed contract with the photographer you select that states the name of the photographer who will actually be taking the shots; all times and places; all dates (those on which all pictures are to be taken, as well as those on which the final proofs, pictures, and albums will be delivered); number and kind of photographs to be taken; who owns the film; all charges for time, travel, and film; and his/her cancellation policy. Remember, your wedding lasts only one day, but the photographs taken will evoke memories that will last for several lifetimes.

PHOTOGRAPHER'S CHECKLIST

Photographer _____

Address _____

_____

Phone _____

Contact Person _____

Interview Date/Time _____

Speciality/Style _____

_____

Special Effects Offered _____

_____

_____

_____

Number of Photographers _____

Number of Assistants _____

Arrival Time/Location _____

_____

Departure Time _____

Pre-wedding Additional Photographs:

1. Date _____

Time _____

Location _____

Persons Required to Attend _____

Dress _____

2. Date _____

Time _____

Location _____

Persons Required to Attend _____

Dress _____

3. Date _____

Time _____

Location _____

Persons Required to Attend _____

Dress _____

Pre-wedding-Day Visit _____

Date _____

Time _____

Location _____

Persons Required to Attend _____

Additional Equipment Required _____

Kind/Location _____

Kind/Location _____

Photos to Be Taken Before the Ceremony _____

_____

_____

Photos to Be Taken During the Ceremony _____

_____

_____

Photos to Be Taken After the Ceremony _____

_____

_____

Photos to Be Taken During the Reception _____

_____

_____

_____

_____

_____

Package Contents _____

_____

_____

_____

_____

_____

_____

_____

_____

Package Price _____

Prices per Additional Photos _____

_____

_____

_____

_____

_____

_____

Additional Charges (travel, film, etc.) _____

_____

_____

_____

_____

_____

_____

Ownership of Film and Proofs _____

Delivery Date of Proofs _____

Return Date for Proofs _____

Delivery Date of Film and/or Album _____

Total Price _____

Deposit Date and Amount _____

_____

Balance Amount and Due Date _____

_____

Notes _____

_____

_____

_____

_____

_____

_____

_____

_____

_____

_____

_____

Engagement Photographs

But there is nothing half so sweet in life as love's young dream

—Clement C. Moore

Some, but not all, brides choose to have their picture taken as soon as they become engaged in order to send it to the newspapers along with their announcement. This should be done as soon as possible, even though it is appropriate for the announcement to appear anywhere from one month to one year before the wedding. Because so many of today's families are so mobile, you may choose to have the announcement and photograph appear in several different cities' papers. It should appear in the papers in the town in which both you and your fiancé reside, both of your hometowns (if different from your current residence and you have not been gone for too long), and where both sets of parents reside.

You may choose to have your picture taken alone, or, as is becoming more and more popular in certain sections of the country, to have it taken with both you and your fiancé. Such portraits can be taken in a studio, or you may choose a location that is more indicative of what the two of you like to do. Even though the photographer is usually required to take the engagement pictures with black-and-white film for the newspapers, you may request that he/she also take several poses in color. They can be used as a keepsake and as gifts for both sets of parents, or they can be displayed at the wedding reception. Discuss the cost of the sitting, the number of poses that this fee includes, and the cost per print for both color and black-and-white. The first print is customarily the most expensive, with repeated prints costing considerably less.

Every newspaper has its own policy and special requirements for printing announcements and photographs. You will need to inquire as to any specifics for deadlines, fees, and type of photo they require (some will accept only black-and-white 8" x 10" glossy prints, for example). Check with the life-style editor of each individual newspaper as to its specific requirements.

You may wish to ask the newspaper some of the following questions:

1. Will the paper allow you to have either your engagement or your wedding photo published but not both? If you choose the engagement photo, it is acceptable to have it appear from one month to one

year before the wedding date, but it is more customary to have it printed six months to one year prior to the day of the festivities.

2. What is the paper's policy on submitting and returning photos after they have been printed? On a piece of paper attached to the back of the photo, be certain to submit the size, the finish, and the specification as to color or black-and-white for the published picture, along with your name, address, and telephone number. Your photo should also be protected by being placed in a large envelope with a stiff piece of cardboard.

3. Make certain you have some sort of contractual agreement stating how much you are being charged by the paper to print your photograph, if anything, and on what day the announcement and the photograph will appear. With some city newspapers, you can request the date on which you would like your announcement to be printed. If you do make such a request, remember that Sunday is always the most popular day, which brings its own set of advantages and disadvantages.

4. With all of the second marriages that occur in today's society, it is becoming more and more common for them to be announced in the same manner as a first marriage—with a photo included.

Your Wedding Portrait

*... The sight of you... is as necessary for me as is
the sun for the spring flowers.*

—M. of Valois

A wedding portrait is a must for most brides and
should be taken approximately one month prior to
your wedding day. You may wish to have it taken in
the photographer's studio, or you may choose a more
relaxed environment such as your home. Some brides
choose to go to the ceremony site and have theirs
taken on the stairs they will descend or in the garden
where the vows will be recited.

At this time you may choose to have your florist make an exact replica of your wedding bouquet in real flowers or you may choose to have one made in silk—in which case, this could be the bouquet you throw to your waiting family and friends during the reception. You may wish to have the wedding salon deliver your dress to the photography site so that you do not have to be responsible for transporting it. Also, you will want everything—makeup, accessories, etc.—to be exactly as they will be on your wedding day. If you wear glasses, you may want to remove them for the photograph. If you feel unnatural without your glasses, you may choose to remove the lenses so that your eyes will show more clearly and reduce glare in the photograph.

Wedding Album Photographs

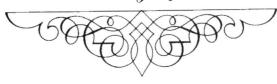

Into all our lives, in many simple, familiar, homely ways, God infuses this element of joy from the surprises of life, which unexpectedly brigten our days, and fill our eyes with light...

—Samuel Longfellow

Long after you walk down the aisle, dance the first wedding waltz, and settle into a life of husband and wife, you can travel back in time at a moment's notice simply by picking up your wedding album. With each turning page, the memories are recreated—the flowers are more beautiful than you remembered; the look in his eye that you did not see as he said, "I do" can be viewed time and time again. These are the pictures that should be captured forever in your wedding album. This list could be endless, but you want your album to tell a story from beginning to end, so there are a few specific poses you will want to be certain to include (and the others are limited only by your imagination).

- you and the groom in a frameable pose

- both of you with the entire wedding party

- you with your bridesmaids

- the groom with his groomsmen

- the two of you with both sets of parents

- you with your parents and another pose with your parents and your closest family members

- the groom with his parents and a second pose with his parents and close family members

- the two of you with both sets of grandparents

- you and your father walking down the aisle

- you and the groom during the ceremony

- the two of you toasting

- the first wedding waltz

- any special decorations or displays

- the two of you leaving at the end of the festivities

Other possible options for wedding photographs are as follows:

- you and your attendants getting ready

- the groom and his attendants getting ready

- everyone as they receive flowers

- individual poses of all attendants

- the groom and the best man

- you and your maid/matron-of-honor

- the groom's grandmother being ushered down the aisle to her seat

- your grandmother being ushered down the aisle to her seat

- the groom's mother being ushered down the aisle to her seat

- your mother being ushered down the aisle to her seat

- ushers escorting important guests

- individual shots of attendants walking down the aisle

- you and the groom kissing

- you and the groom greeting guests

- guests signing the guest book

- the groom's and your hands displaying rings

- your bouquet

- signing the wedding certificate

- the cake

- you and the groom cutting the cake

- you and the groom feeding each other the cake

- toasts

- you and the groom dancing together

- you and your father dancing together

- the groom and his mother dancing together

- the groom taking off the garter

- the groom throwing the garter

- you throwing the bouquet

- the buffet table

- the gift table

- the musicians

- guests throwing rice

- the wedding guests decorating the car

- you and the groom getting into the car

One much asked questions is "Where and when is the best place and time for the photographer to take the specific posed pictures that I want him to take?" There are several options, but you will want to decide a few weeks before the wedding and discuss the time and place with the photographer. Some popular choices are as follows:

- The morning of your wedding you may direct the photographer to go to both your and the groom's homes and take the requested shots of each of you separately and with your family and wedding party. The combined photos could then be taken at the church, or temple directly after the ceremony. If you decide on this option, you must be certain to allow enough time (usually not less than one hour, unless your reception is several hours after the ceremony) and find a quiet place so that guests are not inconvenienced or kept waiting while your pictures are being taken.

- If there is enough time between the ceremony and the reception, you may choose to go to a preselected spot to have the photos taken. This could be at the ceremony or reception site, the photographer's studio, a favorite place of yours and the grooms, or one of your homes.

- If you have no superstitious feelings about the groom seeing you before the ceremony and if your wedding is a less formal one, you may choose to have the family and wedding party arrive up to two hours early and have the photos taken before the ceremony. This option, however, is not possible at a very formal, traditional wedding and may be one that you wish to consider carefully even if your wedding is more contemporary or an informal affair. It is always a moment to remember when the groom sees you for the first time as you walk down the aisle. You should know, however, that the tradition of the groom not seeing the bride before the wedding began with the mythological figure Thor, when it became necessary to keep him from running away in case Freya ,the bride that had been selected for him, was not the beautiful Viking goddess whom he had been promised.

There are several advantages and disadvantages to this option. If taken before the ceremony, you are apt to be less hurried and less hassled by guests, but you probably will be much more nervous; your makeup and dress will likely be perfect, but somehow the photographs will be more "staged"; and even though your fiancé and you probably spent the morning together, there is still something breathtaking about his first glimpse of you as you walk towards him with the music in the background.

• Some couples who have very large, more formal receptions have their formal posed pictures taken right after the guest line is dismantled and the guests are mingling with cocktails before dinner or while they are dancing later in the evening. The important point is to plan the photos for a time when you will be comfortable and will not be keeping your guests waiting.

You will also want to make certain that you inform all family members and participants ahead of time as to which photos they are to be included in and approximately at what time and location they will be taken. You do not want any confusion as to who is to be in which photo or have any delays because one member is unaware that his/her presence is needed.

Family pictures with you and/or the groom will make up a significant number of the pictures you will want to have taken. If you have parents and/or in-laws who are divorced or separated, this can become a very sensitive issue. In these instances, you and the groom will need to decide beforehand exactly who the two of you want involved in which pictures. It is hoped that because this is *your* special day that those closest to you will understand and respect your wishes. The options of which family members and how many shots can be taken are endless. You may choose, for example, to have a series of pictures taken with your natural parents, and then two completely new groups taken with each parent, their spouse, their new son or daughter, and family.

The following guidelines may be helpful:

1. Discuss and decide on who, where, and how many beforehand.

2. Consider carefully everyone's feelings and emotions.

3. Contact the participants before-hand and tell them what you have decided and why.

4. Express that you sincerely hope they will understand and respect your requests and wishes.

Planned Wedding Photography

Planned wedding photography includes those shots taken before, during, and after the ceremony that are usually the most traditional and that are specifically discussed and planned for by you and the photographer. These photographs, when taken during the actual festivities, often suffer several problems. These problems are a result of a lack of time or the inability to find an appropriate place to shoot. Too often the photographer is rushed to shoot the pictures that you have requested and therefore focuses only on the subjects in the camera and forgets how important the background is.

One of the most common problems of cluttered, busy, and clashing backgrounds is when objects seem to be "sprouting" from someone's head, as in the example to the right. The groom seems to be wearing a headdress of flowers in addition to the fact that the draping background is distracting. If this were the only shot of the two of you with either set of parents, you would have been happier if the photographer had more time to select the "perfect" place to shoot.

Consider the background elements.

All brides want traditional posed pictures of the wedding party, parents, the bride and the groom together, etc. You will want to make certain that, wherever these pictures are taken, the background is appropriate and the placement of the people in the picture is pleasing.

There is nothing worse than when the photographer takes a picture of the groomsmen and each one is standing except the two on either end who kneel. The kneeling is unnatural, awkward, and, with the end men kneeling, the proportion is wrong. These types of pictures are the ones that will make you crazy for years because they are so "amateurish."

Traditional posed photograph

Many couples request that the photographer take "posed " pictures that are nontraditional but adapted from traditional poses, as is the example to the right. This couple wanted a picture of the two of them with the groom's parents. They wanted something that would convey the love and the emotion felt during the day but asked the photographer to "pose" something a little out of the ordinary.

This style of photography is becoming very popular and utilizes a technique incorporating the use of depth of field. The mother and father stand behind the couple, slightly out of focus, while the couple stands in the foreground, sharply in focus.

For some couples, this particular style perfectly conveys the emotion and the sentiment of the day.

Creative group posing, using three-dimensional depth

The first page of many traditional wedding albums features a posed picture of the couple's hands, showcasing their new rings. This shot can be taken directly after the ceremony or sometime during the reception. It can be taken with a very sharp focus or made softer and more sentimental by having the photographer use a diffusing or cross-star filter.

This is one shot where you will want to use props to accentuate the hands. You can use your bridal bouquet to rest both hands on, or you may wish to include your wedding invitation or some other object that is very sentimental to the two of you.

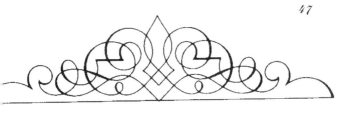

Hand-and-ring pose

Oftentimes you and your new groom will want the photographer to take pictures of such things as your table decorations, the buffet table, certain gifts, or other "still-life" items that you will want to remember and share with family and friends who were unable to attend the wedding festivities.

These scenes need to be planned and arranged by the photographer so that they are as beautiful in the photograph as they were at the wedding. For example, in a photograph, you should almost be able to smell the roses that were in the planters as you and your father walked down the aisle.

Important items in a grouping

One formal photograph that is very popular with many couples is the one that is taken in front of the church or temple where the ceremony is to be performed or has just been performed. Some couples who choose to have their pictures taken in this setting do so several weeks before the actual wedding day so that they may display this photograph during the wedding festivities. This is, also, the photograph that is oftentimes given as a gift to both sets of parents.

If this is one photograph that is important to you, you will want to make certain that the photographer has ample time to shoot. You will want the shot to be simple, elegant, and "posed" to convey the emotion of the moment. You do not want to be hurried so that the two of you appear to be uneasy or frazzled. You will want to discuss with the photographer how important it is that the prop of the church or temple in the background be just "perfect"—with no unnecessary distractions.

Using the church as a background

Candid Wedding Photography

Candid photographs can come from two different sources during the wedding ceremony or the reception. The first includes those that are taken on the spur of the moment when the photographer sees a scene that should be recorded. The second includes the informal shots that are refinements of naturally occurring situations.

Candid shots are the photographs that will tell the true story of the wedding. They highlight certain emotions or certain individuals during special, or not so special, events. These shots should be taken without the subjects even being aware that they are being photographed. If your photographer is as good as he/she should be, he/she will be "invisible" to you and your guests and able to capture moments on film that are truly the ones you will want to remember over and over again.

Photographs taken at times when they are least expected can often be the most fun to share—because these are often shots that were seen or shared by only a few. The photographs of you getting ready are the only way your new husband will be able to share with you the excitement you felt right before the ceremony, or those of guests cleaning-up after the two of you were gone are the only way you will be able to relive the quiet moments when all of the festivities were finally over.

Candid shot before the wedding festivities

You will want to have several of the most important events during the wedding ceremony and reception recorded without your being aware that the photographer is even doing so. You will want to have these memories on film without having to stop the moment and pose for the camera. Posed pictures are fine for certain events; but, the love shared during the ceremony when you give each other your wedding rings or the special way you feel in his arms during the wedding waltz should not be interrupted for any reason.

Candid shot

Candid shot

Truly candid shots are the photographs that are never planned and happen because the photographer just happens to be in the right place at the right time. These are the ones that tell the stories of the emotions that you and your guests experienced and shared.

These are the photographs that will tell you exactly what you were thinking and how you felt. You will be surprised that anyone else saw you at all.

Candid shot

Designing Your Wedding Album

These are the things I prize
And hold of dearest worth...

—Henry Van Dyke

Either ask the photographer to be in charge of designing your album or work with him/her closely to be assured of getting what you want. Images of you and the groom as well as family members should be large, while candid shots or shots of friends or crowds can be smaller. You will want a combination of sizes in your album, as well as some photographs taken at a distance, with others close-up. You may choose to wait until after you have seen the photos to decide which should be large and which small, which should be left full frame and which should be cropped, and which should be combined on which page.

To make your wedding album as special and as personal as it can possibly be, you may want to do one of the following:

- Begin your album with a series of memory pages. These are pages at the beginning of the album which display important memorabilia from the beginning of your relationship to the end of your honeymoon. They might include a ticket stub from the first movie you attended together, a picture of the two of you on the night you were engaged, a copy of your wedding invitation, dried flowers from your bouquet, a piece of lace from your dress, or a plane ticket from your honeymoon.

- Chronicle your entire relationship with pictures and memorabilia. This means taking the above memory pages and inserting them among photographs in their chronological order. For this you may find that you need more than one album because of all of the photos that have been shot and mementos that you have saved and those you will collect during the months before the wedding. This format will allow you the flexibility to insert photos taken by family and friends during special events before the wedding, as well as much loved unexpected shots taken during the ceremony and reception.

You will most certainly want to make gifts of some of the photographs that are included in your album. Traditionally, your parents pay for the costs of the photographer and the videographer as well as all of the prints, albums, and tapes. The wedding album will be a gift to you and the groom from your parents. A thoughtful gesture on your part may be to give the groom a picture of you from the album to place on his desk. (He may wish to do the same for you.) You will also want to have prints made for both sets of parents. At the very least, parents should receive a picture of you and the groom, their immediate family with the newlyweds, both sets of parents together, and the wedding party. It is, however, a much nicer idea to show both sets of parents the proofs and let them select which ones they would like to have. You can indicate how much your budget will allow, and then they can decide if they want to pay for any additional photos. For ease in keeping the finances separate, you may choose to order the prints that will be a gift from you and let both sets of parents order the additional prints they desire directly from the photographer. The prints that are being given as a gift may be bound into a miniature album (which contains ample room for other photos) and presented as a special thank-you for all they did to make your day so special.

Each wedding party participant should also receive a picture of you and the groom and one of the entire wedding party. You may, also, want to let immediate family members and wedding party participants review the proofs and select certain photographs that they would like to have for their own family albums. You will want to make detailed lists of who wants which photos, or you may request that they order any additional prints that are not gifts themselves directly from the photographer.

Wedding Photography & Makeup

That which is loved is always beautiful.

—*Norwegian Proverb*

You will need to discuss your makeup with both your photographer and a professional stylist, if you have chosen to use one. The camera is as discerning as your guests, and you will want to be "made-up" perfect for both. Some recommendations you may wish to consider are as follows: curled eyelashes accented with lengthening, thickening, waterproof mascara (black for brunets, brown for blondes— waterproof so that your mascara does not run down your face if you begin to cry during the ceremony!); oil-control face powder to prevent shine; well-blended and color/complexion-matched foundation (from forehead to decolletage).

Generally, you will do your makeup differently if you are having strictly color or strictly black-and-white photos taken. Color tends to intensify bold shades, so it is advisable to keep your makeup subtle. Stay away from frosted shadows—if a flash is used, they will reflect the light. Complement eye shadow with a smoky shade of liner smudged below the eye, giving the effect of a shadow cast by your bottom lashes. Groom your brows, removing any unwanted hairs that interrupt the natural curve of your eye socket. It is helpful to brush brows upward with clear mascara to hold hairs in place. You will want to highlight cheeks with a wash of soft color that enhances your natural skin tone. Select a color of lipstick that coordinates with your skin tone, dress, and other makeup selections. When applying lipstick, first use a liner pencil to outline lips, smudge this line so that it blends in naturally with the lip area, apply lipstick, blot with a tissue, apply it, blot it, apply it, blot it, until you have a buildup of color with the depth and intensity that you feel comfortable with. This technique will result in a beautiful matte "stain" that will last almost the entire day with only a tiny bit of retouching.

If your photographs are being taken with black-and-white film, you need to be aware that this film whitens pale shades, but darkens rich, vibrant colors. Red lipstick will not photograph as you expect because the film "sees" and reproduces black. You should select most of the same tones of makeup and apply it in the same manner you would for color photography, making just a few modifications.

There is one way to make certain your makeup will look like you want it to in the photographs. Several weeks before your wedding photographs are to be taken, apply your makeup (or have your stylist apply it) exactly as it will be on your wedding day. Then, have a friend take close-up photographs of you with both color and black-and-white film. This will give you time to change colors or techniques if you desire before the big day. If you do make changes in color or application methods, make sure your friend retakes your picture so that you can see if the changes provide the look you are after.

Other Photo Opportunities

£ove indeed, lends a precious seeing to the eye,...;
all sights... are glorified by the
light of its presence.

—*Frederick Saunders*

There are occasions for which you will want to ask family and friends to take photographs on your behalf. And these need not just be at a shower, party, or the rehearsal dinner. Take your camera along when you are shopping with your mother or the brides-maids. Take pictures while meeting with the florist and the caterer for both memory's sake and reference. Shoot family members and friends while they are addressing invitations or preparing the food. These pictures are often as much fun to reminisce over in the years to come as are the pictures of the wedding and the reception.

During more structured events like a shower or the rehearsal dinner, you will want to make arrangements ahead of time for someone to be in charge of taking the pictures. Tell him/her specifically what you would like taken and approximately how many shots. You will be very disappointed if you wanted several roles of film used with a shot of you opening every gift with the giver, but only receive a few candid shots of a limited number of guests. You will want to supply whomever you have asked with both camera and film. Meet with this person a few minutes before the occasion to explain exactly how to use the camera and to practice with a shot or two. Or, if the person feels more comfortable, you can supply the film and he/she can use his/her own camera. In either case, make certain good equipment is used. Professionals recommend a 35-mm auto-focus camera with a built-in flash for both ease and the most professional-looking photographs possible. Make sure that you make arrangements to collect either the undeveloped or developed film at a specific time or you may forget and may never receive your copies of the pictures. All too often, friends forget to get the film developed immediately and then misplace the roll. If family or friends agree to have the pictures developed, make sure they know how many, what size, and which kind you prefer.

A few additional points to help ensure the best "unprofessional" photographs as possible:

1. Try to avoid "bulls-eye" compositions. This means simply focusing on the subject in the middle of the viewfinder without taking into account the surroundings. Try to use all of the picture space by turning the camera to take a vertical shot if it is a better fit. Make certain that the background will not distract from the intended focal point of the picture. Do not shoot a flash camera directly into a mirror or window.

2. Do not try to "pose" subjects or line them up in too straight a line. Naturally "posed" photos are more appealing.

3. Do not have people look directly into the camera. This will prevent "red eye" (that bright red tint eyes appear to have in pictures taken with a flash) as well as make your photos seem more spontaneous and less posed.

4. Be aware of the lighting conditions of wherever the picture is being taken. If you are shooting outdoors, the people in the photograph should not look directly into the sun. Be careful that no one in the shot is hidden by shadows; the lighting needs to be uniform.

5. Make picture taking an event that everyone enjoys—this may not be as easy as it sounds! Have the photographer blend in with the guests, and do not let them know their pictures are being taken. Let everyone pose how and with whom they want, or you may help by getting them involved in the process. For example, pass out disposable cameras as the guests arrive or place a few on the dinner tables. Have everyone take a series of pictures and then return the cameras when they leave so that you can have the film processed. If you have extra prints made of each photo, you can enclose one in each thank-you note you send to those who attended that particular pre-wedding function.

If your budget simply will not allow you to hire a professional photographer and you must call on family and friends, there are several points in addition to the ones already listed that you will want to make certain are understood by your "amateur" photographers.

1. Ask two people to photograph the wedding ceremony and the reception. If there are two taking pictures at all times, there are certain to be several from both that you like very much.

2. Choose people who are more than familiar with the use of a camera— especially the one they will be using.

3. Supply all the film that you want to have taken so that they do not skimp because of their own budget.

4. Follow all of the guidelines that are applicable for the professional photographer: the pre-wedding meeting, the attire, and so on.

5. Check with the clergy to see if there are any restrictions on the use of cameras in the church or temple or during the ceremony.

6. Make a list of important shots that you want each photographer to include, as well as a list of names of important guests that you want to make sure are in several pictures.

7. Take as many "must" shots before the wedding as possible. This will alleviate some of the pressure on your amateur photographers who may have a difficult time remembering all that you want them to shoot.

8. Make certain that they give the rolls of
film to *you* to have developed. It is my
recommendation that, even though it is a
little more expensive, you take the
film to a professional lab to have it
developed. Oftentimes when film is
processed at a one-hour photo lab in a
grocery store or on some other unrelated
site, the developers are not professionals
and the negatives can be scratched,
incorrectly developed, or lost. A professional lab can instruct you as to which
can be enlarged, they can crop the photos
exactly the way you would like to have
them cropped, and they can perform a
myriad of other services that will make
all of your wedding photographs look the
best they possibly can.

Honeymoon Photography

*We can do no great things,
only small things with great love.*

—*Mother Teresa*

When the camera is no longer being used by the professional you hired or by family or friends, there are several points you will want to remember to achieve photos on your honeymoon that are as "professional" as possible.

1. Here again, a 35-mm camera with a built-in flash is recommended for general purposes.

2. You may wish to carry a tripod along for shots that you wish the two of you to be in or those that require a longer exposure than the human hand can hold (a sunset for example).

3. Make certain that you do not skimp on film. *Take plenty with you*—more than you think you will ever need. You want to carry it with you just in case you are unable to find it where you are and when you want it. If you are traveling in a foreign country, it may be much more expensive than you had anticipated.

4. Use 200-speed film. It is the most versatile for a variety of light conditions and provides good-quality prints that can be enlarged with the least distortion.

5. Keep your camera and film separate from the rest of your luggage. It can be lost or it can be damaged when going through x-ray equipment—have it hand-inspected by airport security.

6. If you are taking scenic shots, the best time is either early in the morning or late afternoon when the light is the softest. Remember, however, that the pictures that are the most fun to look at when you return home are those with someone in them—even if you do get tired of having your picture taken in front of everything you see!

7. Use a polarizing filter to enhance the look of scenic shots.

Videography

*A fterward she remembered the times when
she had felt the happiest...*

—*F. Scott Fitzgerald*
Tender is the Night

Traditionally, brides and their grooms have relied on photographers to capture the special moments before, during, and after their wedding ceremony and reception; but, now, with the advent of modern technology, there is a new way to bring back your memories time and time again. Videotaping your wedding festivities will allow you to capture the "essence" of your wedding. You will hear the vows again, and, probably for the first time, see the tears in his eyes and listen to the crack of his voice as he says, "I do." You will see the love and adoring glances, as the two of you dance the wedding waltz. You become a spectator, as with your back turned, you toss your wedding bouquet. You can relive time and time again the emotions you felt, as your dad put his arms around you and kissed "his little girl" good-bye.

A wedding video is becoming a popular means of recording wedding festivities. It is my recommendation that you definitely have a wedding video taken and use a professional to do all of the recording and editing.

Do not use the video in place of the traditional photographs but in addition to them. This is the one place that you will not want to skimp on costs. The videotape of your wedding, if correctly and professionally made, will be played over and over for years to come. It will be the *only* actual record of who was there, what was said, and who did what. For my own wedding, I did not anticipate that this would be as important as it was, so this was where I cut back on my budget. I spent a fortune on the flowers and the food and had an agreeable and most generous relative do all of the videotaping. It is the one and only aspect of my entire wedding that I wish I could redo. Regardless of a friend's or relative's intent, only a professional can give you the quality of taping, the thoroughness that comes from experience, and the "perfectly retold" memories that will be watched for generations to come.

Your videographer's job is a very difficult one indeed. He/she is producing a live film and there will be no retakes. The art of videotaping itself is difficult and complex—add to that the emotions and the chaos of your wedding day, and it becomes even more of a challenge. Every time we watch the video of our wedding ceremony and reception, we wish it would have been handled differently. Not to disparage the job my brother-in-law did, but he had no way of knowing that the sound of the ever so slight wind that was blowing would muffle the words of the officiant, and he did not know how to edit the piece when he was finished to eliminate the footage we did not want or how to add still photographs or background music to make the story complete. So, once again, let me say, "Please do not skimp here!" Save on your budget elsewhere, in which a little creativity will cover up for the lack of finances!

Once you have selected your ceremony and reception sites, you can begin interviewing videotaping companies. You will want to begin this process as quickly as possible—no less than five to six months before your wedding day. Use the same sources that you did for selecting a photographer (see page 9–10).

Once you have selected three possible candidates, follow the guidelines listed below:

1. Make an appointment with each, and allow one hour to discuss the details. Make certain the videographer shows you his/her operation and equipment (a professional should use only broadcast-quality, industrial cameras and ¾" tape). Look for a company that does everything "in-house" rather than one that sends tapes out for editing. Be sure that you take notes concerning all important aspects of the interview. This is such a new area of expertise that you may not understand all of the details and explana-tions to the questions that you ask. If you record all that you think is necessary

during the interview, when you review your notes you may think of other questions that need to be answered or explained.

2. Ask to see tapes of weddings previously recorded and for a description of the proposed agenda for your taping. You may even ask if they will allow you to take one of their videos home so that you can have enough time to review it. This will allow you to make notes and jot down questions and ideas. Again, wherever and whenever you review the tape, you will want to pay attention to the details. Does the videographer videotape with one camera, or use an assistant (or assistants) and tape with two (or more) cameras, editing the tapes together to make a "perfect and complete" version? Do they tape continuously throughout the entire event, editing what is unimportant, or simply tape those events that you request—in which case, they may miss the spontaneous events that are often the most fun to watch. Is the original work done on a Super VHS tape, with your copy being transferred to a regular VHS format? (A master tape on a Super VHS is far superior in quality and clarity.)

Watch for things such as clarity (focus), the steadiness of the video-grapher's hand, the manner in which the videographer moves from one event to another, technical know-how, his/her ability to tape in any light (if yours is a night wedding with candlelight, this may affect his/her ability to tape), voice clarity, importance of events being videoed, and the manner in which he/she gets subjects to respond. Does the videographer make it look natural? Does he/she make those being videoed feel they must perform, which makes most of us very uncomfortable! Does he/she use special techniques and, if so, do you want them used in your video? If they are used in the video the videographer chooses to show you, then they are probably techniques that will show up in your video as well.

You should ask what type of lighting will be used. Does the videographer have a new low-light camera? Does he/she solve the problem of harsh glaring lights by using a method called "bounce lighting." Here, a large floor light is aimed at the ceiling and the reflection illuminates the area without direct light shining onto the guests.

In regards to clarity of sound, most experts agree that wireless remote equipment is the optimal method for those occasions where it is imperative you hear every word that is spoken. At the ceremony, for example, recording the vows can be guaranteed by placing a small microphone under the officiant's clothing or the groom's lapels. At the reception, a camera-mounted mike will do an adequate job.

In addition to observing the video-grapher's equipment and techniques, you will also want to make note of his/her personality. You will want to select someone who has a pleasant personal-ity—someone who will listen to what you want and with whom you, your wedding party, and guests will feel comfortable. Some videographers can be very overbearing in their demands and offensive to those they want to tape. This, again, is one provider of wedding services who will spend a great deal of time with everyone involved with the festivities; so he/she should be someone who you and everyone else will like and feel comfortable with.

3. Ask for references and take the time to check them. This will be your best single indicator of how your videos will turn out.

4. Discuss the type of production you want. Can the videographer work with the photographer? Can music be dubbed into the tape? Will the videographer let you select the music you prefer? Is he/she able to add names, titles, quotations

made by guests, being careful not to overdo the effects? Will the film be edited? If the film is edited, will you be able to be involved in the editing and will he/she give you the raw footage? (Some of the moments you will think are the most important or the funniest may end up on the cutting room floor if you do not rescue them.) Because this is such a new area, make certain to ask for the videographer's suggestions and recommendations in regards to all phases of production.

5. Does the videographer offer a package, and what does it include? Most professionals feel that an edited tape totaling forty-five minutes of viewing time is adequate to cover the "best" moments of the wedding. Few people, other than you and the groom, will want to sit through a three-hour tape of your wedding-day activities! If you do not feel forty-five minutes is long enough you may wish to ask for a fifteen minute highlight tape (which most videographers will supply at no additional charge). You will also want to check to see how many additional tapes the package includes. You may want extras for family and wedding party participants, and you will certainly want to have at least one additional copy of your own in the event something happens to the one you are viewing; they

often get "eaten" by the machine, or the tape could break after several viewings.

6. Make certain the videographer visits the actual ceremony and reception sites prior to your wedding date to check for any obstacles and restrictions on videotaping. If your budget will allow, you may even ask him/her to tape the rehearsal so that he/she is familiar with the obstacles and the sequence of events. This way, there will be no surprises the day of the wedding that will prevent him/her from taking footage of the ceremony that you have requested.

7. Go over the time of the ceremony and the reception, and the locations for both (indoors or outdoors can make a considerable difference to a videographer). Make certain he/she agrees to be one of the first to arrive and one of the last to leave (along with the photographer), videotaping during the times you feel are important. Some of the very early or final clean-up footage after you have gone may be some of the most treasured.

8. You should give the videographer the same pertinent information that you give the photographer. He/she will need to know the number of people in the wedding party, the style of your wedding, your wedding colors, the timetable of events, and anything else you may feel is important.

9. The videographer should meet with you, the photographer, and a preselected friend or relative a day or two before the wedding. The purpose of this meeting is to give a detailed list of the events you wish to have on video to the videographer, and introduce him/her to a close friend or family member who will identify important guests and family members that you wish to have included in the taping. This is the person to whom he/she will be able to ask any questions during both the ceremony and the reception. The person you select will need to be certain that both the photographer and the videographer know where he/she is seated during the ceremony and will need to make themselves easily accessible to both before all festivities, during and after the reception.

You may want to request certain "special" moments to be included in your video. For example, the videographer could meet with both you and the groom separately before the ceremony, at which time you both can offer a wish or a prayer to your partner. This could become one of the most treasured gifts you could receive as you view the tape in the years to come.

You may also request that the video-grapher "interview" certain prearranged guests so, they can bestow a special wish on the two of you or offer a poem or prayer. You should ask those you want included well ahead of time so that they have time to prepare what they would like to say or if they decline, because they just do not feel comfortable granting your request, it will give you time to ask someone else.

You may also ask that the video-grapher tape a small amount of footage at each table. This will give you the opportunity to see everyone in atten-dance even if you did not have time to speak to them all.

10. With the videographer, discuss the attire that you wish him/her and any assistants to wear. Again, if you request something out of the ordinary, you will need to discuss who will pay for the rental or the purchase of the desired garments. If you are having a theme wedding and a costume will make him/her feel uncom-fortable, you will need to reach a solution that satisfies you both.

11. Make sure the videographer you speak with will be the one who actually takes all of the footage during the entire wedding event. You do not want to interview one person with whom you have placed your confidence only to find someone else doing the work.

12. Check to see if the videographer works with assistants—one who helps with the equipment and a second or third to take additional footage in places where the main cameraman may not be.

13. Ask if he/she carries an extra camera just in case something goes wrong with the one he/she intended to use. If not, what is his/her solution should such a problem arise?

14. Discuss the fee. Does the videographer charge a flat fee or by the hour? Is there an additional charge for pre-wedding meetings? How much footage is included in the fee? What would the fee be if during the festivities you decide you want additional events recorded? What is the additional charge for editing, dubbing, and other features? Is there a travel fee? Is there an overtime charge if he/she is required to stay longer than expected? Is one day of the week or time of day more expensive than others? What is the fee for each additional tape that you will want for family and friends?

15. What deposit is required? It is a good idea to place your deposit on a credit card, protecting yourself by special consumer protection laws should something go wrong with the video that you both agreed to in writing.

16. You may wish to work out a payment schedule for the video. Since this is something that you may not have planned in your budget, perhaps there is some type of arrangement to pay for these services over a longer period of time.

17. What is the videographer's cancellation policy in regards to your cancelling or his/her cancelling? What is his/her alternative plan if it becomes necessary for him/her to cancel?

18. Does the videographer guarantee the quality of his/her work? Who makes the decision as to whether or not the quality and the content are what was agreed upon in the case of a disagreement?

19. You must have a detailed contract with the videographer you select that states the name of who will actually do the taping, all the places (and times) where he/she is required, all dates (those on which all videos are to be taken as well as those on which the final tape is to be delivered), all charges (for time, travel, film, etc.) as well as the cancellation policy. Remember, your wedding lasts only one day—but the video will be watched for years to come.

VIDEOGRAPHER'S CHECKLIST

Name _____

Address _____

Phone _____

Contact Person _____

Interview Date/Time _____

Videographer's Style _____

Arrival Time/Location _____

Number of Videographers _____

Number of Assistants _____

Events to Be Videotaped _____

_____

_____

_____

_____

_____

_____

_____

At Home _____

_____

_____

Before the Ceremony _____

_____

_____

During the Ceremony _____

_____

_____

Before the Reception _____

_____

_____

During the Reception _____

_____

After the Reception _____

_____

_____

_____

Departure Time _____

Pre-wedding Meetings _____

_____

_____

_____

Date _____

Time _____

Location _____

Persons Required to Attend _____

_____

_____

Type of Equipment Used _____

Type of Tape Used _____

Hours of Raw Footage _____

Who Owns Raw Footage _____

Videotaping Service _____

Editing _____

Sound Dubbing _____

Special Effects _____

Additional Equipment Required _____

Kind/Location _____

Kind/Location _____

Miscellaneous _____

_____

_____

_____

Additional Tapes _____

Number _____

Cost per Tape _____

Delivery Date of Videos _____

Total Cost _____

Deposit _____

Other _____

_____

_____

Taping Events Without a Professional Videographer

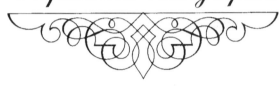

In order that people may be happy in their work, these three things are needed: they must be fit for it; they must not do too much of it; and they must have a sense of success in it...

—John Ruskin

For those events before the ceremony that you may wish to have videoed, you probably will not want to hire a professional. You will, therefore, probably ask the assistance of a friend or relative to tape the occasions that you feel are important, such as the engagement party, special showers, or the rehearsal and rehearsal dinner. These, too, are events that are a joy to relive again and again.

To help make these videos as professional as possible, you may wish to follow the guidelines below:

1. Make arrangements ahead of time for someone to be in charge of the video camera during the event. This person should be very familiar with the camera before arriving. If this person has a camera of his/her own, he/she may wish to use it and have you buy the tapes. Or, if he/she uses yours, he/she will need to practice before the final taping so that they feel confident and comfortable.

2. Tell the person in charge, specifically, how much you would like him/her to tape and what and whom you would like included. You do not want to find, for example, at the end of the evening, that there is ten-minutes worth of the evening's highlights when you were hoping for a thirty minute tape.

3. Regardless of who supplies the camera, you should supply all of the film. Select a good-quality tape. A reliable video cassette will last much longer than an economy one.

4. Make certain the videographer moves the camera *slowly* and steadily. He/she may wish to use a tripod whenever possible to avoid jerky movements.

5. Have the videographer vary the shots. He/she should use long angles that capture the guests of honor surrounded by friends and family, medium ones that bring the action closer, and close-ups that show the emotion and mood of the moment. Close-ups should be taped for a minimum of five to ten seconds. The tape time will seem like forever, but when you view the tape it will provide the needed time to "see" who is being taped and help avoid sudden jerky movements.

6. You may suggest that the videographer "interview" some of the guests. To make them feel more at ease during the interview, the videographer should ask "open-ended" questions. He/she should not ask questions like "Do you have something you would like to say to the bride and groom?" This will only cause the interviewee to "freeze." Instead, questions should be asked that require a direct answer. For example, the video-grapher could ask the mother of the bride what she remembers most about the night when the young couple announced that they were going to be married. Or, the videographer could ask the father of the groom what he most likes about his new daughter in law.

7. The person doing the taping needs to be aware of the back lighting. He/she needs to make certain that the necessary light is coming from over his/her shoulder, not from behind the people being taped. Otherwise, you will end up with silhouettes rather than well-lit video images.

8. Make sure he/she tapes only on "slow speed", which produces the highest-quality taping.

9. Discuss who will supply batteries. You need to have backups if the camcorder's battery will not last for several hours of taping.

10. Have the videographer shoot plenty of tape. Remember, you can edit and record over the tape if you do not want it and a moment missed can never be recaptured.

11. Have the videographer be as inconspicuous as possible. Most guests will feel very uncomfortable if they know their movements and emotions are being taped.

12. Make arrangements to collect the tapes at the end of the party or at a specified time later on. If you do not, you may forget. Months later, when you remember that you asked someone to tape your wedding festivities, the tape may have been lost or recorded over by mistake.

These "home movies" will mean as much to you, your children, and your grandchildren as any other you will take during your lifetime. Plan ahead, be prepared, and try to economize on your budget in other areas.

This is your one and only opportunity to record one of the happiest times of your life. It is a record for generations of family members to enjoy.

Index

The farther backward you can look, the farther forward you are likely to see.

—Winston Churchill